B E Y O N D
T H E   B O T T O M   L I N E

We believe there are alternatives to the prevailing economic and business wisdom. We think there are other ways to organize the economy and workplaces, ways that will not sacrifice social prosperity or the environment, and which will be more in tune with human needs, not profits.

Let's ask questions, create new models, and learn from our efforts to introduce change. And let's dare to dream.

Alis Valencia
EDITOR

EX
LIBRIS

SAINT
JOSEPH'S
COLLEGE
RENSSELAER
INDIANA

B E Y O N D
T H E   B O T T O M   L I N E

DO WE REALLY WANT
CONSTANT CHANGE?

Theodore E. Zorn
Lars Thøger Christensen
George Cheney

BK

BERRETT-KOEHLER COMMUNICATIONS, INC.

Berrett-Koehler Communications, Inc.
450 Sansome Street, Suite 1200
San Francisco, CA 94111

Beyond the Bottom Line (ISSN 1526-3177) is a bimonthly booklet series published by Berrett-Koehler Communications, Inc., 450 Sansome Street, Suite 1200, San Francisco, CA 94111. Subscriptions: $49 for one year (six issues). Send orders to Berrett-Koehler Communications, Inc., P.O. Box 565, Williston, VT 05495-9900, or call 800/929-2929, or order on-line at www.bkconnection.com.

Editorial correspondence: Address editorial correspondence and inquiries to Alis Valencia, Editor, 18875 Trillium Lane, Fort Bragg, CA 95437, or call 707/964-7964, or send e-mail to avalencia@bkpub.com.

Printed in the United States of America
on acid-free recycled paper.

Beyond the Bottome Line no. 2
ISBN 1-58376-076-8

CONTENTS

Preface   vii

1. The Glorification of Change   1

2. What Is Organizational Change?   9

3. Organizational Responses to the Change Imperative   15

4. Consequences of Our Obsession with Change   27

5. Restoring the Balance Between Change and Stability   35

Notes   39

Discussion Starters   45

About the Authors   47

PREFACE

A bit of humor recently passed around the Internet was a list of items titled "Work in Corporate America." The list was prefaced by this statement: "You know you work in corporate America in the nineties if . . ." It included such responses as "You've sat at the same desk for four years and worked for three different companies," "Your company welcome sign is attached with Velcro," "Your resume is on a diskette in your pocket," "The company logo on your badge is drawn on a post-it note," and most tellingly, "Change is the norm."

As is often the case, colloquial humor provides an insightful commentary on current conditions. What is it telling us here? First, that organizations have embraced change and flexibility with a passion; second, that one consequence of this is that workers are more mobile, and perhaps more disposable, than ever.

As we approach the end of the century, we want to stop and reflect on some current trends—and to point out that some very important things have changed in our workplaces. The particular change we want to focus on is change itself—and especially our attitudes toward change. It's not that change is anything new in society. Many people have experienced upheavals, dislocations, and technological revolution. What's different today is that we are experiencing *constant* change and its related disruptions.[1]

The common wisdom in much of the popular management literature—what we might call the dominant management discourse—is that organizations must change, and they must do so *continuously.* According to this discourse, one important way in which they must try to change is to become more flexible and adaptable, which of course prepares them to deal with subsequent changes. Change and flexibility have become "god terms"—terms that are accepted unquestioningly as good. All you have to do is invoke them and you can gain the ready assent of others. In this way, the term *change* functions a lot like the terms *quality, efficiency, dialogue,* and *customer service* in managerial discourses today: lots of things are done in their name, and it's difficult to criticize anything done under one of those labels. The celebration of change has become more and more pronounced in recent years. Interestingly, what we see happening in the workplace is both a microcosm of and contributory to larger cultural trends. It seems that change, flexibility, and adaptability have become increasingly prominent as business and social values.

The trend is perhaps the strongest in the United States, where the cultural premium on the future has always been greater than regard for the past. But we see much the same orientation toward change showing up in other industrialized countries, including those in Europe and East Asia as well as Australia and New Zealand. Yet in addition to the pitfalls of overemphasizing change and flexibility at the expense of stability, routine, commitment, and loyalty, organizations actually may not be able to embrace change in the all-encompassing and continuous mode suggested in the prevailing change discourse. The downsides to constant change are relevant to business, families, neighborhoods, and society in general. And there are some important ironies rarely considered by those who promote change programs. Many organizations that claim to value change and flexibility, for example, often practice the opposite. In this booklet, we will discuss the emergence of change as a business and social value, and illustrate the human consequences and organizational ironies of change management programs. Finally, we'll make some recommendations for balancing the opposing, but equally valuable, forces of change and stability.

— ✐ —

We would like to get your feedback on what we write. We can all be reached by e-mail: Ted Zorn at tzorn@mngt.waikato.ac.nz, Lars Thøger Christensen at ltc@sam.sdu.dk, and George Cheney at gcheney@selway.umt.edu.

I

THE GLORIFICATION OF CHANGE

Pruning minutes and seconds and hundredths of seconds has become an obsession in all but a few segments of our society. In the spirit of Olympic swimmers shaving their chest hair, television networks are ever so delicately shaving the "blacks"—the punctuation marks between shows, when the screen fades momentarily to darkness. Brooke High School in the northern panhandle of West Virginia tries to save one minute per class break and thus welcomes its students to the age of speed.... Yet we have made our choices and are still making them. We humans have chosen speed and we thrive on it—more than we generally admit. Our ability to work fast and play fast gives us power. It thrills us.... Instantaneity rules in the network and in our emotional lives: instant coffee, instant intimacy, instant replay, and instant gratification.

—James Gleick[1]

To begin, let's be clear about our point of view: we do not oppose change, either in business or in other sectors. There are good reasons why managers value change. Trying new things is how we learn. It's also exciting, energizing, even thrilling to explore a previously untried way of doing business, to improve practices and to grow. Stability and routine can be, well, boring. Then there's the obvious fact that things around us change and we have to change with them in order to adapt. Managers see competitors move into their markets, they observe changes in sales figures or government funding, or they witness new technology and its applications emerge. The facts of increasingly global markets and the resulting increases in competition are well documented.[2] So managers seek to adapt, as they should. What we're suggesting is that change has become almost an obsession—that maybe we've gone overboard in the extent to which we value it. In this way, we can get tangled up in a web of our own weaving, trapping ourselves in a race that we do not always understand.

Although the two cannot be completely separated, we want to distinguish change as a means to an end from change as a value in and of itself. Managers have always looked for ways to change and improve organizations (as have most other policymakers), but in recent years *change itself* has become the preeminent focus and value. Management has long been subject to trends and even fads, beginning with what was termed scientific management early in the twentieth century and continuing to the present preoccupations with continuous improvement and total customer service. Every management trend or program features some value or values, even if these aren't always spelled out. In the last decades, management has embraced fashions in which the highest value was productivity (with management by objectives [MBO] in the 1970s), excellence and quality (total quality management [TQM] in the 1980s), and customer service (in the 1990s). In each case, organizations attempted to change in various ways to reflect these values. Now what's primarily valued is change itself, along with complementary values like flexibility and adaptability.

Let's explore the evidence for this claim. Some researchers have suggested that highly valued phenomena in a society give rise to a proliferation of terms to describe or label them. By this measure, today's managers worship change. Think of all the recent terms used for radical organizational change: reorganization, restructuring, reengineering, reinvention, transformation, business process integration, business process improvement, organizational renewal, organizational development, delayering, downsizing, and rightsizing. Although there are important differences, all of these buzzwords add up to changing the organization in fairly dramatic ways. At the heart of each is the idea of making change the norm. Continuous improvement, or what the Japanese call *Kaizen,* is perhaps the best example. The assumption behind endorsing continuous improvement is that we must be constantly changing our work processes—that even excellence (to borrow a 1980s buzzword) isn't good enough. As one writer said, "perpetual innovation" is what's needed.[3] Sadly, though, when implemented *Kaizen* usually focuses almost exclusively on productivity and not on people.

The current rage about change transcends the specific interventionist strategies of MBO, TQM, or business process reengineering (BPR) in its embracing imperative. Under the banner of change, we should not rest, wait to test the results of last year's initiative, or appreciate the value of routines. There may be sound reasons for a specific intervention. However, such programs are attractive in part because they are consistent with the change ideal. And as a result, we are telling each other to change more often, faster, and more comprehensively. The change ideal thus becomes like a hammer in a child's hand: it gets used on everything in sight, whether it fits the job or not.

The evidence that we are elevating change as a value certainly doesn't stop there. Check out the bookshelves or the local business school course offerings. The rise of academic studies in "change management" and organizational development, along with the growth in the numbers of journals, books, and courses devoted to these topics, is dramatic. The glorification of change is absolutely rampant in popular management books and articles. For a number of years, management guru Tom Peters was the foremost proponent of these ideas. His book titles, such as *Thriving on Chaos: Handbook for a Management Revolution,*[4] *Liberation Management: Necessary Disorganization for the Nanosecond Nineties,*[5] and *The Circle of Innovation,* all scream out the glory of corporate change. Peters's management film series, which includes a film called *What Have You Changed Lately?,* implores managers to look continually for things to change. His "revolutionary" imperatives for management include slogans like "leadership that loves change," "constant innovation in all areas of the firm," "practice purposeful impatience," and "an obsession with responsiveness." His conviction that change is not simply a condition but a "must-do" leads him to make such statements as "If you are not refiguring your organization to become a fast-changing, high-value-adding creator of niche markets, you are simply out of step." Today, other gurus are making their appearance on the change scene, but the overall message is the same. Consider the title of another hugely influential management best-seller, Hammer and Champy's *Reengineering: Handbook for a New Management Revolution.* Or Bill Gates's recent *Business @ the Speed of Thought.*[6] Each of these titles conjures up images of dramatic change and quick adaptation. Be nimble and quick, embrace the turbulence, and change: the message that we are supposed to see these as exciting, as "opportunities," is crystal clear.

Such books are quite consistent in their message about the need for constant change. For example, a recent best-seller proclaims: "The level of competition today requires high levels and continuous improvement of organizational performance in four critical areas: the quality of goods and services, the cost of producing goods and services, the speed with which products and services are brought to market, [and] innovation in the development of new products and services."[7] Similar arguments are made for public sector organizations. For example, "The kind of governments that developed during the industrial era, with their sluggish, centralized bureaucracy, their preoccupation with rules and regulations, and their hierarchical chains of command, no longer work very well. . . . [They] simply do not function well in the rapidly changing, information technology–intensive society and economy of the 1990s."[8] If we add to these books the number of management courses and seminars that take for granted the need for constant change—and aspire to help us become even more change-oriented—we arrive at an image of a corporate world that is awash in change. Indeed, a recent marketing conference in Europe featuring Philip Kotler and Joey Reiman was advertised with this heading: "Do your feel your company is being chased by wild animals? If not, you should!"

Yet another example. One of Andersen Consulting's fastest-growing business units is Andersen Contracting, promoted as "helping its clients create customized, flexible workforces." Andersen Contracting produced 32 percent of Andersen Consulting's revenues in the Australia–New Zealand region in 1998.

In a way, the current romance with change is a natural extension of modernity's faith in progress. Since the Renaissance, and especially following the Enlightenment of the late eighteenth century, the human capacity to engineer and reengineer the world has been celebrated, at least in the occidental world. Today, we have the power and tools to do more of that—to bring about radical changes in our environment, in society, and in ourselves. And as we illustrate in this booklet, the celebration of change has intensified in a number of important ways. This celebration, however, is not unambiguous. In contrast to the modern idea of progress, the contemporary notion of change is based on a far less clear idea about where society is, or should be, heading. This uncertainty, sometimes referred to as the *postmodern condition,* pervades all aspects of society and endows our activities with doubt and disorientation. Where progress used to be the beacon, we now talk about growth and development. And where the former reflected a vision of improvement and betterment, *growth and development* simply refer to the process of change itself. Thus, the notion of change that we celebrate today goes hand in hand with doubt and uncertainty about the meaning of life. Change, in other words, is heavily crisis-prone. However, the rush to change has become so fast, so heated, and so unthinking in many cases that we rarely have time to reflect on our work lives, let alone the deeper meanings of notions like progress, growth, and development. Although we may not always realize this, change becomes a problem when it turns into change for change's sake—then change is ruling us, rather than vice versa. And we suffer the results with faster-paced work environments and high-speed living that scarcely gives us time to notice how much of life we're missing.

CULTURAL BOREDOM

So glorifying change is not just an isolated management phenomenon. It is part of a larger cultural phenomenon of valuing change. There seems to be a sort of cultural boredom in which we can't be tied to tradition or satisfied with the present. Who wants to be old-fashioned when you can be cutting-edge? Who wants the status quo when the possibility of something better is just around the corner? Unfortunately, as we'll discuss shortly, the questions "Change to what?" and "For what?" may well get lost in the rush toward change. It's like the question of efficiency. We have to ask "Efficiency for what purpose?" and "In what ways?"

A recent *Time* magazine cover story argued that Americans are taking more risks because of the relative lack of risk for most people in contemporary society.[10] The article documented increases in people voluntarily changing jobs, practicing dangerous sports, engaging in risky sexual activity—and the list goes on. The argument is that recent economic prosperity, lack of high-risk conflicts (global wars), and daily boredom all may make taking risks—such as large-scale corporate change—seem safer and, at the same time, more energizing and thrilling. Although this argument may seem a bit simplistic, it captures well how change today is closely related to a crisis of meaning.

For more evidence of the glorification of change, consider politics. Try to find an example of a political campaign in which the challenger (and often even the incumbent) does not use "the need for change" as a key campaign platform! "It's time for change" is a fairly safe platform for any candidate these days. Bill Clinton exhorted the American public in 1992 by insisting, "What we need is change!" Governor George W. Bush of Texas, currently the front-running candidate for the U.S. presidency in 2000, does his share of this as well. Check out the language used on his campaign Web site: "The world is changing, and so must the attitude of government." "Governor Bush envisions a different role for government." And he envisions "the next bold step of welfare reform."[11] Interestingly, even so-called conservatives, who traditionally saw themselves as protectors of the past and present, now advocate change. Today it seems fully acceptable to preach change for change's sake, often without specifying what sorts of policy changes are desired.

Vice President Al Gore represents the incumbent party in the White House, yet in the current environment he can't afford *not* to align himself with change. His campaign agenda is rife with such phrases as "economic growth through innovation" and "revolutionary change in education."[12] Paradoxically, he represents a continuation of the Clinton administration—which at this writing still gets high approval ratings—but in a culture that worships change, he can't afford to claim to represent "more of the same." That sounds too much like stability. Also, the message of "same old . . ."

wouldn't serve to enhance Gore's lackluster image. Of course, candidates for public office have always emphasized how they can do better, but today's campaigners clearly talk up change in a way that presumes it to be a value. "Change" and "progress" become vague abstractions that need only to be invoked and seldom explained. When they are discussed in more specific terms, it is usually in terms of an unbridled faith in technological advancement—as in Al Gore's celebration of the Internet as a solution to many of society's ills.

There is an undertone of impatience in political discourse and on the part of the media, almost as if those institutions are mirroring the breathtaking speed at which the computer industry moves. Initiatives and programs are criticized when they're barely sketched out, let alone implemented. Slogans come and go as quickly as fashions in athletic footwear. Remember the Republican Party's 1994–95 Contract with America? The media feeds a general craving for novelty, which is perhaps best seen in the rapidity by which political and other celebrities rise and fall. So media figures from Newt Gingrich to Madonna are showered with attention for a short period, then quickly become old news. And public opinion polling during the height of U.S. presidential campaigns is now conducted up to three times daily—as if a change in mood signified a substantial change in opinion.

INSTANT GRATIFICATION

Even more disturbing, perhaps, is that we have come to equate instantaneous response—to consumer market research and public opinion polls—with a deep form of democracy.[13] Although this idea is spelled out most explicitly in marketing, where responsiveness to external demands is the raison d'être of the discipline, we find today that this ethos of marketing has influenced most sectors of society.[14] As a consequence, a change program that claims to be grounded in external demands has a strong rhetorical advantage. In creating so-called responsive institutions, we have bypassed careful reflection and meaningful discussion. This is as true in business as it is in politics, the media, and sadly, often the home.[15]

If you aren't convinced yet, look at how popular films and television shows portray change. The media, of course, often reflect contemporary values. For example, in the recent movie *Pleasantville*, two 1990s teenagers find themselves transported back to a 1950s *Ozzie and Harriet*–type television show, where nothing much ever changes. Dad says, "Honey, I'm home" every evening upon return from work and finds his dinner on the table, prepared by his smiling wife, who welcomes him together with their squeaky-clean kids. In the black-and-white world of Pleasantville, the 1990s teens gradually introduce new ideas and challenge old ones. When individuals embrace change, they become transformed (and appear in color rather than in black and white). For a while, there's a lot of conflict because the transformed individuals are introducing changes. One of them is even tried in court for doing so. In defending himself, he says, "I know you all want everything to remain pleasant. But there is so much that's better." For the audience, the message, once again, is clear: we may find the stability of the past nostalgic, but life is better if we go for change.

In addition to the media's explicit messages about change, the portrayal and encouragement of instant gratification by the media feed our impatience with the present and our desire for change. As critics have noted for many years, half-hour sitcoms in which crises emerge and then are solved—not to mention thirty-second commercials that do the same—create a false impression of the way most of life's problems are addressed. And although we should not necessarily expect sitcoms and commercials to reflect life as it is, such portrayals may feed a desire to get quick satisfaction, whether through purchasing a product, ending a relationship, or "reinventing" an organization. In any case, long-term solutions requiring patience and endurance are devalued in our media-saturated and novelty-hungry world.

The need for energizing thrills in a low-risk era and the media's influence certainly both contribute to the obsession with change. So too does the frequency of news about new technological breakthroughs and the availability of "new and improved" technological products. For example, a few years ago, cloning was science fiction to most of us. We now know that it's been successfully accomplished with several different species on several continents. The number of mobile phones just recently surpassed the number of fixed telephones in Italy, and the same will likely happen in other countries by the end of the year. And of course, a new computer is hardly out of the box before one that is faster, with more features, comes to market. A "generation" in the computer industry is now understood as less than six months. Thus, we are bombarded with new technologies allowing for radical new possibilities. Some of these trends lead to dissatisfaction among users of these products, but it's not surprising that we accept rapid and radical change as normal in other spheres of life, too.

Finally, the pervasive penetration of the business or market model into all spheres of life also contributes to the emphasis on change. Institutions that used to distance themselves from business now grasp this model with passion. Thus, churches, universities, and hospitals—and sometimes families and individuals—have mission statements, strategic plans, and slick ads and promotional campaigns. The hugely successful Covey Group—that's Stephen Covey of *Seven Habits of Highly Successful People* fame[16]—encourages participants in its seminars to create personal and family mission statements and then hold family meetings to craft, apply, and revisit the mission. Many churches today have developed "marketing plans" to recruit new members. Not surprisingly, internalizing the business model into other spheres of life often brings with it the business obsession with change. So churches, universities, families, and relationships also begin thinking in terms of reengineering, continuous improvement, and "keeping up with the race"—perhaps the dominant metaphor in talk about change. Thus, the influences driving this obsession with change are many and complex.

2

WHAT IS ORGANIZATIONAL CHANGE?

Let's stop for a moment to reflect on the idea of organizational change. What do we mean when we talk about organizational change, and what are our assumptions about it? Where do these assumptions come from? It may be useful to make a few careful distinctions here about the nature of change.

A curious management phenomenon is that we often accept a management trend or value without being clear about just what we're buying into. This certainly happens in the case of change, although it's not unique to it. People are vague with lots of things they value, and that's not altogether unreasonable. Being vague allows us to agree in general that something is important, while also allowing for quite a bit of flexibility in how it's interpreted or implemented. For example, how many organizations have bought into teams or teamwork without really specifying what that means for them? In our own consulting practices, we have sometimes been asked by an organization to do team building or to implement team-based reorganization. But when we ask the policymakers what they envision and why they want it, they often can only say, "Well, we know that teams are good things, and we gotta have them." In some cases, the change to teams is just a change in labels: "You used to be a department. Now you're a team!" In other cases, implementing teams results in more substantial changes in the ways work gets done. But the ambiguity of the concept does mean that it's useful to stop and reflect on just what we intend when we say we're for change. Often, all that managers can say about their need for teams is that they like the idea based on their personal knowledge of organized sports.

Most important value-based concepts that inspire us or bring us together are ambiguous. Think of how *freedom* or *democracy* or *equality* functions in political discourse, both to unite people under certain banners and to gloss over certain differences. Today's popular corporate and business slogans function much the same way. Who can be against *dialogue?* Or *quality?* Yet on the specific meanings of these terms as applied to work processes, products, and services, we may have lots of different ideas. Thus, dialogue seems to refer to anything an organization of today does in order to relate to its various audiences, including advertising in mass media. Likewise, TQM has come to mean many different things, with some having little to do with W. Edwards Deming's famous fourteen points. Yet what's important for many public as well as private sector organizations is that they use the language and label of TQM, almost regardless of what their specific practices are. Although such ambiguities are a fact of language and life, we should be aware of what's going on under a big symbolic umbrella like *change*.[1]

Broadly speaking, organizational change refers to any alteration or modification of organizational structures or processes. Obviously, however, there are important differences in the kinds of organizational changes managers pursue. Organizational change has a number of dimensions. We can distinguish it in terms of degree (how much things really change), whether it's primarily externally or internally driven, and whether it is material or "discursive"—that is, mostly talk. (But as we've already shown, the talk *itself* can be quite important in how it directs our attention toward certain goals or values.) We will discuss these characteristics in Chapter 3. But first, more broadly, change can be understood by its order of magnitude—whether it is first-order change or second-order change. We can also understand the idea of change better if we consider its opposite—stability or permanence.

MAGNITUDES OF CHANGE

Change can be major—a restructuring, for example—or minor—a change in a customer feedback form, for example. Change can also be immediate and abrupt, as when layoffs are announced, or long-term and gradual, such as what often occurs after benchmarking or employee suggestion programs.

For analytical and practical purposes, it is useful to distinguish between what American philosopher Gregory Bateson called *first-order and second-order changes*. We can think of these as general categories. First-order changes—sometimes referred to as "changes in order not to change"—are minor, incremental changes that any living system has to make in order to avoid the more fundamental second-order changes.[2] Consider, for example, driving a car on a winding country road. In order to avoid ending up in the ditch, destroying the car, and possibly being injured (second-order changes), the driver has to make continuous adjustments with the steering wheel (first-order changes). Another example is the way a chameleon's skin changes in color when its surroundings change. These changes are necessary for the chameleon to avoid a more fundamental change—being eaten by an enemy. As we observe with these examples, first-order changes are adjustments that involve only certain parts of the system. And these parts are only "loosely coupled"—or loosely linked—with the rest of the system.[3] If they were tightly coupled, the rest of the car would have to turn as much as its wheels do, and the chameleon would have to change as radically internally as externally.

As the examples indicate, second-order change is unusual and more difficult to monitor by the system itself. A second-order change occurs when the entity becomes something fundamentally different from what it was. Although second-order change is contingent upon events and crises outside the system in question, it is not directly deducible from such external forces. Second-order change, then, is neither necessary (in the sense of being inevitable or preordained) nor continuous (that is, a long series of small steps within the entity in process). Change, in this fundamental sense of the term, cannot easily be planned for. Sometimes, second-order changes cannot be anticipated at all, even when they are a result of several first-order changes or adjustments.

In work organizations, minor, incremental, first-order changes happen every day. Someone is hired, fired, or promoted. Business forms or work processes are tweaked. A policy is revised. Second-order changes—at least in the extreme—happen less often. A government agency is eliminated. A company goes bankrupt and no longer exists. A new company or type of organization rises up from the ashes of an old one. An organization adopts a wholly new goal. Thus, in second-order change, different parts of the system are tightly coupled to each other and forced to change simultaneously and in concert.

Most managers would probably say that the changes they pursue are somewhere in between first-order and second-order change. Such in-betweens include reengineering organizational operations, developing new products and services, and devising a campaign to change the corporate identity. These sorts of changes are often quite significant to the organization—more than the first-order changes described earlier—but less dramatic than second-order changes. But managers often talk about and seek to implement organizational change by framing it in fundamental terms. That is, terms like *reinvention* and *transformation* suggest the kind of dramatic, fundamental change we associate with second-order changes. Yet what actually changes is often far less than that. Changes in image, in identity, and in positioning are often given these labels that suggest more radical change.

Let's make another distinction here: change versus innovation. All innovations are changes, but not all changes are necessarily innovations. So the term *change* is broader, more general, than the term *innovation*. Innovation implies a new idea, product, or practice, whereas some changes could involve reviving an old idea or reverting to a previously discarded practice.[4] We can also distinguish the two terms in the ways in which they have been treated historically by managers. The current interest in change seems broader, more embracing than the usual notion of innovation. Although innovation has always been valued in organizations, it was treated quite differently from how change is treated now. Innovation was something that the research and development (R&D) department was responsible for. It was contained, controlled within the bureaucracy. It was "located" in a particular area of the organization. Executives didn't want just any manager making major changes. In the command-and-control world of the organization that existed before the 1980s, most managers were expected to carry out executive orders, not to come up with their own.

Today, though, things are different. Executives not only say they want individual managers to make changes but also expect it as part of the manager's job. In effect, every manager is expected to be a change agent—constantly improving, experimenting, and reinventing. "Every manager an entrepreneur" is the idea today.

Change becomes a sweeping imperative that the whole organization is talking about and presumably doing. Beyond this, in fact, all employees are being asked to see themselves as entrepreneurs at the level of their jobs. And that is a sound imperative in many respects.[5]

CHANGE VERSUS STABILITY

To understand the nature of change, it is also helpful to consider its opposite: constancy, permanence, or stability. We can view change versus constancy as a *dialectic*, which means that the two ideas are in a sort of natural tension.

Change and constancy are mutually dependent and both desirable, but they also try to cancel each other out. They are interdependent, in that we can't have one pole without the other. We can't imagine change without considering permanence, and vice versa. This we saw clearly in our earlier examples of changes made in order not to change. Thus, for the chameleon or the driver of the car, stability and change are inseparable. In organizations, this dialectic is at play whenever a change is followed up by stabilizing measures—for example, when a new identity program is consolidated with a design manual or when new ways of handling customer complaints become part of the organization's standard operating procedures. Change makes sense only against the standard or the backdrop of stability, yet it is often discussed today in a way that is "free floating," almost without reference to anything else.

So, there is always a tension between the two that organizations constantly grapple with. In fact, it's a basic tension that organizations must manage. This tension can be productive, but it can also be disruptive. Organizations want a measure of stability. The very structure of an organization is built upon having some policies or standard operating procedures, reliable methods of decision making, action programs, and dependable sources of expertise and knowledge. This is true even if the organization is not very bureaucratic but rather more of an "organic network," where there's a high degree of coordination and flexibility and the organization is relatively "flat." Indeed, in order to retain a sense of coherent identity, organizations need to balance change with stability.[6] The idea of core values or mission, for example, which is so popular today, also attests to the not-so-often acknowledged merits of stability and permanence.

But of course, organizations want change too, and often for good reasons. In some organizations' experience, the more they emphasize permanence and stability, the harder it is for them to carry out a departure from their practices. Tradition in such cases not only becomes a source of pride but also something that constrains choices. Think of IBM in the 1980s. One of its pillars of tradition was service. Another was its tradition of secure employment, which served its reputation well and made it a sought-after place to work. But that tradition also constrained choices when the company felt forced to change in the face of a rapidly transforming computer market. Then the multinational giant found itself violating to some extent both of these fundamental principles while it tried to reinvent itself: it made massive layoffs and for a time was unresponsive to market demands.

Conversely, the more an organization strives for continuous change, the more difficult it can be for members to feel a sense of stability, especially when the changes in question do not follow logically or organically from established missions and strategic plans. Too much change often makes a period of relative stability more attractive—even though managers rarely allow themselves to say this out loud. For example, after a rapid succession of proposals for new programs in the Waikato Management School (Hamilton, New Zealand) this year, many staff members wanted to call a moratorium on new proposals! So caught up are many universities today with the idea of evaluating performance and working toward change that the act of making proposals itself becomes a key work activity, pulling faculty and staff energies away from more basic tasks. Similarly, after restructuring, many business organizations find that fundamental changes need to be followed by periods of stability where the changes are implemented and consolidated into organizational practices.

Stability is what allows organizations and people to be flexible and to explore the world and themselves. In their personal lives, families, couples, and individuals constantly seek a balance in the dialectic between change and stability that is right for them at the time. But there is an ebb and flow as they seek change, then stability, and so on. We're suggesting that perhaps this dialectic is out of whack in the workplace today. In some respects, we may have elevated the value of change over constancy to an unhealthy level.

3

ORGANIZATIONAL RESPONSES TO THE CHANGE IMPERATIVE

Organizations pursue changes for a variety of reasons. Sometimes change is implemented wholly or largely because of internal concerns, such as the perceived need to revitalize or motivate people, or to address problems, inefficiencies, or opportunities for improvement. And of course, sometimes managers often have multiple reasons for making changes. But most often today, managers pursue change in the name of responsiveness to external forces. Thus, organizational change can be provoked by a competitor's launching of a new product or service, a bold prediction about the emergence of a new market, or a decline in employee loyalty or morale.

The argument about the need for radical and constant change today is primarily based on the observation that the environment in which contemporary organizations operate is becoming increasingly turbulent—that is, it is changing rapidly, unpredictably, and in multiple ways. This is so for a number of reasons. First, the globalization of markets has resulted in the lowering of barriers to the free flow of trade and capital and thus has increased competition, with many firms finding new competitors from distant lands right outside their doors. Listen to well-known consulting firm McKinsey's take on this: "Over time the only class that matters will be world-class. All others will be forced to restructure or go out of business."[1] Although they cite the example of some companies that are making the necessary changes, most, they say, are moving too slowly. Of course, developments in technology also contribute to the turbulence because they enable new products and new ways of doing business in a global market. By relying on e-commerce, start-up businesses and other organizations whose scope might previously have been limited to a particular geographic region become competitors for organizations that previously had a stable and predictable market.

Second, a culture of investment, where money managers and financiers put tremendous pressure on corporations to change their corporate strategy midstream, is also becoming more pervasive. For example, noted Wall Street mutual funds wizard Michael Price is known for having pressured Chase Manhattan to merge with Chemical Bank in the late 1990s. Especially significant about this case was that, in commanding hundreds of millions of dollars in stock shares, Price was able to force Chase to abandon its longtime commitment to avoiding layoffs and providing generous benefits to all segments of its workforce.[2] In this way, new networks of investors and representatives have emerged as power brokers that can demand massive and instantaneous shifts in corporate strategy or policy. This is part of a changing corporate climate, where ever more distant decision makers can shape or shake the actions of a corporation, using stock value as the chief criterion for assessment and armed with the claim that they represent hundreds or even thousands of big- and small-time investors.[3]

Third, customers not only are demanding more variety and faster service but also seem to be more fickle in their attitudes, opinions, and product choices. This disloyal and demanding attitude, however, is not confined to customers. It reflects a more general position among stakeholders of all sorts, who are now described as more savvy than ever, and sometimes more political as well. Thus, government and not-for-profit organizations are facing increasingly demanding taxpayers and sources of funding that require that such organizations do more with less, while business corporations in many sectors of society—especially tobacco, chemicals, and oil—are experiencing increasing stakeholder demands for openness and environmental and social responsibility.

The recommended management response to such pressures is to organize for continuous change. That is, become a flexible organization that can react and respond quickly to changes in the environment—even if this means abandoning traditional product lines or announcing a new statement on core values.

TALK ABOUT CHANGE

Now, just because people agree on the need for change, sing its praises, and even claim to be initiating changes doesn't mean everyone's actually doing it.

Our talk about change is not necessarily the same as change itself (although, we reiterate, this kind of talk is important). Boasting to colleagues or running an ad campaign about how your division has "reinvented itself" is quite a different thing from making changes in products, services, or work processes. This is what we mean when we say that change may be primarily discursive rather than material. Although our language is generally very powerful in creating the world we live in, it is also possible that the discourse of change itself can be a way for organizations to avoid changes in a more fundamental sense. So, it's useful to explore this "talk" about change in a bit more depth.

Our talk often reflects conflicting assumptions about change. Sometimes we talk about change as if it is something we can choose to do and therefore have control over. The idea behind benchmarking and continuous improvement programs is that we can initiate and manage change. Similarly, organizations today put a great deal of energy and money into "change management." In our consulting work, each of us has been asked to help organizations learn how to manage change better on many occasions. From this standpoint, change can be learned in a seminar or harnessed with the right program.

At other times, people talk about change as if it is something they have no control over, as if it is something that happens to them—for example, when they talk about a specific development being "inevitable." When the three of us have discussed the changing nature of the university system (especially the trend toward universities becoming more market-oriented, or businesslike) in the three countries we hail from, each of us has been told that these changes are the "wave of the future" and that we must simply accept and adapt to them. Many of the changes occurring in the U.S. health care system are also described in these terms, making it hard for individual hospitals, clinics, or health maintenance organizations to stake out independent positions on values, policies, and practices.

Employees in university, health care, and other sectors are required to attend seminars on "coping with change" that many times suggest a kind of helplessness in the face of change that runs counter to the idea of managing their organization's change and future. But seldom are such contradictions explored.

In another example, the Clinton administration successfully employed the image of "a rising tide that will lift all boats" in 1993 to 1994 to promote the latest GATT agreement and the expansion of free trade in the Americas through NAFTA. Coupled with this phrasing was the idea that those who didn't ride the wave would be swamped. Similarly, a manager told one of us that "change is like riding a bicycle. You have to keep moving or you'll fall off," suggesting that we have no choice but to change organizations, even though from his perspective it may seem as if we have a choice in how we change.

CRM Films, of Carlsbad, California, has produced a number of videos about change. One is called "Riding the Wave: Strategies for Change." A preview video says: "Workplace 2000 is going to mean one wild breaking wave after another, from fluctuating feedback and changing roles to shifting priorities and stiffer competition. Attempt to control all this unbridled turbulence and you're likely to wipe out. Instead, learn to tap into the exciting energy of change, and catch the ride of your life, with CRM's new video." Another video from CRM is even more interesting, from our standpoint. It's titled "The Power of Future Conversation." The promotional blurb claims that "80 percent of our conversations are focused on the past" and cites this as a problem. The video is designed to retrain people "to achieve extraordinary results by simply turning conversation away from the past and into the future."

As we've said before, messages about the value of change are flooding the environment. Managers and executives hear these messages and contribute their own. This creates an interesting cycle of events, as managers feel the pressure of the discourse valuing change. This discourse pushes them to create changes—or at least to seem to be doing so. In other words, we have come to see a competent manager as one who is constantly experimenting, looking for new opportunities, and running with new trends and fashions. Sometimes the result is material, or concrete. For example, the organization is reengineered so that positions are eliminated, jobs are lost or outsourced, and different people acquire new responsibilities. At other times, the changes are more talk than action. For example, the CEO announces that the organization is a customer-responsive organization or that departments are now "teams," although not much is noticeably different. In yet other cases, we may not even be able to determine whether the changes referred to are substantial or mere talk.

Still, we can refer to change as happening on at least three levels, which run from various kinds of first-order changes, or changes-in-order-not-to-change, to the more substantial second-order changes.

Mostly Talk

The discourse that celebrates change at the level of vision, mission, and slogan is a mostly talk kind of change. It "floats" above. Although it is an important point of reference for the organization, it has no great effect on work processes or daily activities. The discourse is highlighted whenever managers or employees attend training seminars, read popular management books or magazines, or chat with fellow Rotary Club members about current events in their organizations. Change is seen as something "we care about and do," but the concrete evidence of this to an outsider is limited beyond the change-oriented talk. Still, the talk itself may occupy a great deal of work time and energy. In addition, ironically, it may increase employee insecurity rather than strengthening the resolve and confidence needed to effect real changes.

Limited Change

The organization adopts the popular managerial discourse on change, but the prescribed policies and practices are modified according to "local" knowledge and organizational tradition. In this case, the discourse does penetrate daily work activities, but the scope of actual changes may be limited to certain departments, functions, or practices. And the changes may take a form that is not typical for organizations in the same or another industry that adopts such a program. Thus, total quality management, like total quality control before it, has come to be a mantle that organizations take on while pursuing a variety of different programs beneath it. In some cases, TQM is adapted to the organizations' specific purposes; at other times, it is a kind of rationalization for doing what the policymakers intended all along.[4]

Substantial Change

Here, the discourse about change leads to significant alteration in work activities in the organization far beyond the domain of the training seminar, and in ways that subordinate the organization's local knowledge and traditions. Thus, change occurs in a manner generally consistent with the architects or authors of the particular program of change, or at least in a way commonly understood by most practitioners of the program. Still, even at this level of change, there are at least three important dimensions of difference:

- The change may be localized to certain parts of the organization, or it may be universal.

- The change may be restricted to certain work practices, or it may be embracing and thoroughgoing.

- The change may be implemented but not pursued or evaluated, or it may be followed up and assessed.

For example, BPR may involve a significant reordering of work processes around core activities, such as procurement, development and production, and customer service, in ways that eliminate traditional departments or replace them with flexible, multidisciplinary work teams. But even in this case, we must be alert to differences in implementation across organizations. Some organizations may adopt the idea of reengineering in part to seem to be cutting-edge and alleviate their own guilt for not having been up on a previous management trend.[5]

Obviously, there's a direct link here to the discussion in Chapter 2 about magnitude of change. Given the desirability of change and the pressure to appear to do something fundamental and to do so continuously, the incremental adjustments that we called first-order changes—"changes in order not to change"—are often presented as second-order changes. And many times this results in concrete changes, sometimes because the minor changes add up and produce unexpected side effects. Thus, because managers implicitly understand the difficulty and dangers in continuous radical change, despite what the prevailing discourse tells them, they often engage in the discourse to manage their individual and organizational impressions but do relatively little in the way of significant change.

New Concepts of Leadership

Even the way we talk about leadership now reflects the preoccupation with change, coinciding with the ways in which we now think about the role of manager in this change-obsessed era. Leadership used to be taught in management schools as "influencing others toward goal achievement." Do you remember any of those leadership seminars you went to that used *situational leadership* or *leadership styles?* In them, we learned that leadership was basically good management. It was providing direction and support to influence people to strive for effective goal accomplishment. Situational leadership theory, for example, taught that leadership involved matching the level of direction and support with the follower's developmental level in order to create a situation in which the job got done correctly.[6] So leadership was just effective supervision—simply influencing people to do their existing jobs well. In practice, models such as these did little to encourage innovation or experimentation. Rather, they encouraged managers to do a better job of carrying out directives from above—primarily to maintain the status quo—but to do so more efficiently.

Not any more. Leadership has been reconceptualized since the mid-1980s to mean creating change, all the time. Think of the models and terms we're seeing now, such as *transformational leadership* and *visionary leadership*. It's pretty much accepted wisdom in leadership studies today that *leadership* refers to the process of creating change, whereas *management* refers to the process of creating order and stability. Take noted Harvard Business School professor and popular management writer John Kotter's definition of leadership: A process of producing change through establishing direction, and aligning, motivating, and inspiring people.[7] Like most other contemporary theorists and popular business writers, Kotter is quite explicit in viewing leaders as change agents.

Of course, much of this writing—both academic and popular business—has denigrated management in order to elevate leadership. And interestingly, the criticism of past practices and past wisdom seems to be the built-in logic of most management books today. For example, Edward Lawler calls the need for effective management "old logic." He goes on to say, "In the new logic, leadership, not bureaucratic management, is central." We need fewer managers and more leaders, we're told. But, the story continues, there's a lack of leadership talent (read: people willing to attempt dramatic change). Here's Lawler again: "Although 95 percent of American managers understand the logic of the new leadership . . . only 5 percent of them can practice it."[8] All glorify the value of change—and, of course, pave the way for more demand for change management consultancy.

This shift from viewing leadership as effective supervision to creating change reflects in part the larger cultural shift toward elevating the value of change. It also reflects dissatisfaction in academic circles with inconsistent research findings from the "old" theories and dissatisfaction in management circles with the lack of applicability of such theories to executive-level positions that are more about strategy than supervision. And with change management becoming a highly lucrative business, the continuous rejection of established theories and perspectives has become almost institutionalized. Often, theories get more attention if they're proclaimed to be "breakthroughs" or "clear departures from received wisdom"—in other words, totally new. Another important influence has been in recognizing that traditional theories of organizational leadership seem far removed from the way we talk about great historical leaders, such as Gandhi, King, or FDR, who were often considered great in large part because of their role in creating change.

CEOs and other managers know what we consider to be great organizational leadership today. They know that their reputations are based on creating change, or at least appearing to do so. Look at any company's press releases, CEO speeches, or annual reports. The message from the CEO is bound to emphasize a commitment to change. Listen to Michael Andrews, CEO of New Zealand's Fletcher Challenge: "We are moving quickly away from reliance on large-scale, capital-intensive businesses where it is difficult to differentiate customer solutions for value. We are now pursuing ways of extracting more value from our existing operations with minimal further capital commitment. . . . We have begun this shift already."[9] And this is a company that attempted to restructure annually during most of the 1990s!

At this point, we are not questioning whether making these changes is a wise strategy. All we're saying is that this kind of language—proclaiming bold, aggressive changes—is typical, almost necessary, because of the pronounced expectation for leaders to create change. To oppose change or not to endorse it makes one a "dinosaur."

It's no different for midlevel and even lower-level managers—they too know they must be seen to pursue change aggressively. One of our recent research projects focused on a small staff department in a New Zealand city government. The department manager bought the book *Nuts!* (which talks about the business practices of Southwest Airlines) as a way to stimulate change in the department. He took his small staff on benchmarking trips, had them make presentations on change ideas, applied for and won a New Zealand quality award, and constantly exhorted his staff to do more, to innovate, to try harder.[10] No manager in today's climate can afford to appear just to get the work done, even if it's done well.

A PROACTIVE MARKET ORIENTATION

Because the need to change is most often attributed to radical and turbulent changes in external environments, most organizations today find themselves working hard to decipher what the future of their markets and other environments will be like. Thus, many organizations conduct opinion polls or market analyses regularly in attempts to "read" and understand the winds of change. However, as many organizations have come to realize, the market cannot tell them much about which kind of changes to embrace themselves. Although organizations overload themselves with information that demonstrates growing consumer dissatisfaction, increased competition, the significance of new technologies, the proliferation of products and brands, shortened product life cycles, and increased pressures from policymakers and interest groups, these same organizations are usually uncertain about what exactly to do to in response. And here the typical management ideals and prescriptions of customer satisfaction, service, quality, innovation, creativity, and flexibility offer only limited guidance.

As a consequence, a growing number of organizations seek to define and enact changes themselves, often in advance of any actual changes in their environment. This is essentially what *being proactive* means. Rather than wait for specific demands to come from their surroundings, proactive organizations delineate their own standards for change and thus hope to set the agenda for the changes in their specific industry. As a Danish marketing manager told one of us, being proactive means "being at the forefront of the development we expect." Thus, organizations are trying desperately to get on top of change before it happens, all the while preaching customer responsiveness and adaptation to the will of the market.

How can organizations do this? Obviously, since they often read the same books, participate in the same management seminars, and hear the same predictions about the future, managers have a tendency to expect the same change scenarios to unfold around them. This is quite clear when we interview managers about their visions of the future; such visions are remarkably similar across organizations. Still, proactivity means more than predicting change. Proactivity means seeking to regain control of the change process by imposing change on oneself. Organizations usually do this by becoming flexible in a limited number of domains. Some car producers, for example, allow their customers to design their "own" car out of 160 available options.[11] Volvo has just made it possible for its customers to do this over the Internet. Similar strategies are followed by producers of pagers, mobile phones, clothes, and so on. The basic idea behind this strategy is to define flexible measures in order to remain stable in other domains.

Although this may be possible in principle, the constant efforts of organizations to control their own process of change has a tendency to produce new and derived forms of change that cannot be controlled so easily. For example, when Tom Peters in *Thriving on Chaos* tells us that the marketplace is becoming more and more turbulent and chaotic and urges managers, in order to keep up with the changes, to add at least ten value-increasing differentiators to each product or service every ninety days, he forgets that such small changes produce bigger changes and that there is a business environment where turbulence is produced by the very same companies that are trying to escape it.[12] Thus, predictions may well turn out to be self-fulfilling prophecies.

IRONIES IN THE PURSUIT OF CHANGE

As we've seen, organizations often try to balance change and flexibility with stability or persistence. However, there's a paradox here in that sometimes—and perhaps often—organizations in practice seek the opposite of what they profess. For example, research has shown that many organizations boldly profess their use of change-oriented programs like TQM but change very little about the way they operate. One in-depth study of TQM implementation showed that managers often cite as evidence of their TQM "success" projects that were not originally part of the TQM program. The same study showed that in spite of ignoring most of the tools and procedures of TQM, managers tried to maintain the myth that they have implemented major changes.[13] Why? In part, to show their own influence ("I made a difference!") and in part because of the legitimacy they and their organizations gain by being seen as innovators—leading change. Of course, all organizations do certain things or organize themselves in certain ways because such actions help them gain legitimacy in their markets. Clearly, the more strongly the ideal of change is pronounced, the more important it becomes for organizations to appear flexible and adaptable—that is, to communicate change with powerful, suggestive symbols. Many change programs, including TQM and BPR, can be understood in these terms. Interestingly, in the logic of the change discourse, such symbols and legitimizing actions may actually help organizations establish a buffer between their organizational routines and the changes in their surroundings.[14] That is, they can carry on producing products or delivering services in the way they know and not be distracted by trying to learn new procedures. Corporate success stories about elaborate change programs, for example, are often used by other managers to justify adopting those change programs, even when those stories are largely based on fiction, as in the TQM study described here. So the momentum gathers, at least for a while. In this way, many change-oriented programs operate like banners under which the organization can quietly go about business as usual.

This strategy is appealing simply because organizations—especially companies in the same industry—like to mimic one another. At times, it may seem that they deny their own "local knowledge," the hard-learned lessons, and simply jump on a bandwagon without really knowing where it's headed. At other times, such strategies are adopted purposely as a change-in-order-not-to-change strategy that allows the organization to appear cutting-edge while continuing business as usual. As we have suggested, many proactive change strategies do indeed have this dual purpose: to make sure that the changes the organization embraces are at once new and adaptive to external needs, and at the same time, are part of the organization's own repertoire of standard operating procedures. The producer that allows customers to design their purchase from available options thus combines flexibility and stability in an interesting way that makes it possible for it to be responsive to external demands while also avoid making more fundamental changes. In such situations, it may sometimes be difficult to see what is change and what is not.

In fact, the all-encompassing imperative to change, as touted by Tom Peters and others, is impossible for an organization or a society to sustain. For one thing, it overlooks the human need for stability. For another, it demands that organizations continually throw themselves into a state of chaos. The message is, "Whatever you are doing today should be disrupted, discontinued, and replaced." This notion is not only absurd but also ignores how important stability and predictability are for organizational efficiency. Therefore, it's hardly surprising that many organizations covertly develop strategies for containing change and securing some stable operations—all the while hopping aboard the change bandwagon.

4

CONSEQUENCES OF OUR
OBSESSION WITH CHANGE

Up to a point, valuing change, flexibility, and adaptability is a good thing. Both poles of the dialectic are desirable, as we have seen. Growth and learning imply and require change. And we must all be flexible and adaptable enough to deal with new situations. It's the treatment of these as god terms or unassailable goods, the lack of reflection when considering them versus stability or routine, that we see as the major problem today. Let's look at what we lose when we elevate the importance of change too highly.

The hard consequences of the past decade's change frenzy may look pretty good from the perspective of some people. The U.S. economy has experienced eight years of sustained growth, in part, many would argue, because businesses have pursued change-oriented programs. Recent reports by the U.S. Department of Commerce and Bureau of Labor applaud corporate restructuring and the new flexible approaches to work processes, employment patterns, and networking with other firms in various industries.[1] But the effects of continuous change—in the forms of downsizing, restructuring, and outsourcing, especially—have been pretty grim for many other people. Millions have lost jobs and taken lower-paying, part-time, or temporary jobs. Recent figures show that the fastest-growing segment of the American labor force is made up of those who work for temporary agencies. Indeed, the agency Manpower is now the largest employer in the

United States.[2] Not surprisingly, the gap between rich and poor in this country has grown dramatically, just as it is also doing in the United Kingdom, Germany, Australia, New Zealand, and other nations that are undergoing similar economic upheavals.

Recent U.S. opinion surveys show widespread feelings of insecurity about the future at the very same time that people see the economy as booming.[3] At the University of Montana, where one of us teaches, students make poignant observations about the conflicting trends in a course called Communication and Quality of Worklife. They can see how the health of the economy must be assessed on multiple levels, and they ask why they don't feel good about the future at a time when the Dow Jones Industrial Average is well above 10,000. So, certain indications of progress resulting from change are in a way divorced from the experiences of common people. The "economy" can become something of an abstraction that, ironically, is separate from our daily experiences, thus contributing to the crisis of meaning and direction that we mentioned earlier. And the phrase "just business" can be used to justify all sorts of dramatic business and governmental policies that may serve the interests of some rather than benefit the many.[4]

Because change is an accepted good, the "need for change" can often be used rhetorically to do the objectionable. That is, if you want to persuade people to take some action today, a good persuasive strategy to use is to invoke change. "We've gotta keep up with the times," you might say. Or, "You can't stand still, not in this competitive environment." It becomes a convenient strategy to use as a rationale for eliminating jobs, moving factories offshore, and supporting other questionable practices. Not only managers and the media but often also people on the street, unreflecting, portray these practices as "difficult but necessary adaptations to an increasingly competitive global market."

In fact, anyone who would resist change in today's organizations is at a tremendous persuasive disadvantage. The person or group advocating change often doesn't need to provide a rationale, but the skeptic may be called "resister," "obstructionist," or even "organizational terrorist!"[5] The weight of presumption lies so heavily with the change promoters that there's scarcely any debate. This is certainly not democracy, and it's not good business practice either.

One consequence of repeated downsizings, ironically, is the shortage of "executive talent." That's right. We've glorified change, and as a result apparently don't have anyone left to create more of it. The 1998 American Management Association's Staffing and Structure Survey showed that middle management has for years been disproportionately targeted for elimination as companies continue their quest to become "lean and mean." So who is left to take the top jobs? A 1999 *Management Review* cover story was entitled "The Death of Executive Talent." The article quoted a top human resources consultant, who said, "Downsizing has meant that companies no longer have developmental roles, like assistant or deputy jobs, from which people were traditionally promoted."[6] The article also mentioned several times that while we have more MBAs than ever, we have fewer leaders (read: change creators).

And what about the use of resources to create change? The change imperative often means bringing in consultants. Because of the obsession with change, companies spend untold sums on outside change agents who will help them put in place the latest fashion, even when the success rate of the program is marginal. You think we're exaggerating? Well, the international management consulting firm Price Waterhouse Coopers estimated the global market for just one of those fashions—business process outsourcing—at $80 billion in 1998 and expected that to double in the next five years. And the firm boldly sell its benefits: "BPO does what process reengineering and downsizing failed to do—lower costs and increase productivity (while boosting employee satisfaction)."[7] But note what PWC is also recognizing: that last year's fads—reengineering and downsizing, which, by the way PWC was a strong proponent of and made millions selling—were largely *unsuccessful.* As American sociologist Richard Sennett said eloquently: "It became clear to many business leaders by the mid-1990s that only in the highly paid fantasy life of consultants can a large organization define a new business plan, trim and 'reengineer' itself to suit, then steam forward to realize the new design. . . . Most reengineering efforts fail, largely because institutions become dysfunctional during the people-squeezing process: business plans are discarded and revised; expected benefits turn out to be ephemeral; the organization loses direction."[8]

Beyond these rather concrete consequences of our obsession with change, what about the moral and spiritual effects? We quote Sennett again: "The most tangible sign of change might be the motto 'No long-term'. . . . 'No long-term' is altering the very meaning of work. . . .' Jobs' are being replaced by 'projects' and 'fields of work.' " No long-term, says Sennett, "is a principle which corrodes trust, loyalty, and mutual commitment."[9]

Thus, what often appears on the surface as a new dynamic form of organization may be in part an organization that doesn't value its own accumulated wisdom, keeps all its employees on the edge wondering "what

.

next," and devalues the kind of expertise that is developed over the course of a person's entire career. For all the hoopla over high job satisfaction in work teams, says Sennett, some of these groups turn out to be pretty superficial when it comes to the kinds of bonds that are formed between employees.

Let's step away from the workplace for a moment. Take the glorification of change down at a personal or family level. Most of us see the value of stability and routine in our daily home life. Any parent knows its value in raising children. There are some obvious ways that changing for the sake of change wouldn't be acceptable for most people. Changing spouses or changing a small child's schedule are a couple of obvious ones.

Speaking of the effects on families, John Gray, political adviser to Margaret Thatcher, observes a huge contradiction between the New Right's embrace of unbridled free trade with rampant market changes and its desire to maintain traditional family units and neighborhoods. Gray sees nothing more opposed to stability in the home and community than an ever-expanding and changing market with few controls.[10] For an unbridled market thrives on change and tends to work in opposition to tradition. The quest to open up new markets, networks of communication, and new avenues of consumption not only tends to globalize certain experiences but also can undermine efforts to hold onto local distinctiveness and autonomy.[11]

At the societal level we find other contradictions, too. Although change seems unavoidable in a dynamic world, it is important to realize that often change is reduced to, and seen as, "turbulence"—a condition often created by the frantic activities of organizations themselves. As we suggested in Chapter 3, by constantly projecting their own expectations about the future onto their surroundings, contemporary organizations tend to precipitate the uncertainty that they try to escape.[12] In consequence, the market and the entire business culture vibrates nervously to the intensifying beat of the consultant's drum.

In a sense, we are better educated about the reasons for change today than we are about the benefits of stability. We come to accept job mobility and the temporariness of relationships as the order of the day. The social contract between individuals and organizations is framed by both parties as weak and transitory. With our current bias against stability, we fail to appreciate the kind of expertise and knowledge that gets built up over years in a profession as a person's skills are honed—after all, wisdom is born of experience. Ageism also figures in here. Companies in most industries today won't touch anyone over age fifty, and many will not even consider employing a person over forty. We also fail to see the value in long-term, trustful relationships in the workplace, in alliances making up the larger market, and in activities that sustain our communities. Ironically, the market's drive toward change may well undermine the very kind of trusting relations it needs to flourish—just as the Austrian economist Joseph Schumpeter predicted over fifty years ago.[13] Financiers and stockholders demand that organizations restructure and streamline their practices, often with short-term profit uppermost in mind. In an interesting recent article in *The New Yorker*, John Cassidy presented an example of how market pressures, especially as framed internally by young executives, can be used to oppose tradition in ways ultimately harmful to a firm.[14] In this case Goldman Sachs, a century-old New York investment banking firm, decided in 1999 to go public with stock sales, thereby abandoning its partnership form. Cassidy argued that the firm's long-standing emphasis on stable, trusting relationships—both internally and with clients—will be jeopardized. Loyalty to the company and its ideals and practices, along with lasting relationships with clients, will take a backseat to making a quick buck and to shifting loyalties on the part of investors (including both executives themselves and outside purchasers of stock). Cassidy cited Schumpeter, saying that an ever-expanding market may well undermine its own foundations as it swallows up the very kinds of relationships on which its institutions depend.

How Employees Respond to Continuous Change

How do employees react to all this change? They're often overwhelmed. Almost thirty years ago, Alvin Toffler wrote the book *Future Shock,* which alerted us to the idea that the pace of change is increasing.[15] Toffler warned about the potential for people being overwhelmed by change—stressed, burned out. As consultants, we've certainly experienced this "change fatigue" with people we've worked with in corporations, hospitals, universities, and governmental agencies.

Not surprisingly, many employees resist major organizational changes. Part of the reason is simply because of the frequency of change programs—what might be called the "flavor-of-the-month" response. Every time another change program is marched out as *the* solution or "the wave of the future," employees' cynicism is pushed up another notch.

This is precisely why even the most well-intentioned programs can run into opposition. Employees weary from this year's initiative legitimately wonder whether the next round of training seminars will leave them much time just to do their jobs. There's also deep-seated questioning of the motives, goals, and authenticity of any program when employees suspect that there will be no follow-up. Much of an organization's resources and workforce may be mobilized toward no positive result, and cynical veterans may ignore or actually try to undermine the next program that comes along. Sabotage is not unthinkable in such circumstances.[16] At the very least, a lot of energy and time is spent nervously wondering and discussing the changes, as one employee in a company that went through multiple restructurings suggested: "Everyone was trying to figure [the impending layoff] out. When you went on break it was not unusual to find over thirty people in the smoking area talking and talking about it. We wasted more than 140 years of salary in all the time that was spent talking and arguing about what was going to happen. No one could do any work."[17]

When management abandons TQM and embraces reengineering, then abandons reengineering in favor of business process outsourcing, many employees just shake their heads. And sometimes they do a bit more to get in the way of the new program's success. They may argue to give the old program more time to be successful, insist on retaining some parts of the prior approach (possibly diluting or limiting the effectiveness of the new one). Or they may compare the new program with previously unsuccessful programs ("It's just like when we tried quality circles a few years back"), convincing others of their skepticism about its likely success.[18]

Research on effective change management itself points to the dangers of too much change. Indeed, one of the key characteristics of successful change programs is persistence—in a sense, the opposite of change.[19] Organizations that change in a "knee-jerk" way promote cynicism. Those that "stay the course" are more likely to bolster their identity and win employee support. Plus, there will be an opportunity to test a new initiative, see some results, and evaluate its future prospects. Employees balk at major changes because there's a common theme to many of the most popular change programs: people lose their jobs. What makes it worse is that management, and the high-priced consultants they bring in to "help," often frame the changes in upbeat or soothing language. Price Waterhouse Coopers, for example, touts its BPO program as "a win-win proposition for both the organization and its employees—and . . . it really empowers the employee." Yet, the firm defines it as "the long-term contracting of a company's noncore business processes to an outside service provider." Someone may be getting empowered, but someone also is losing a job in that equation. In another press release, PWC cites the results of a survey of top executives of organizations that have used BPO to outsource their human resources management units.

These executives "believe that BPO enables them to: focus on core competencies (96 percent), achieve greater efficiency *without having to invest in people* and technology (91 percent), become more profitable (85 percent), and provide better service levels than internal departments can provide (66 percent)."[20] Sounds like a dream solution, doesn't it? But notice the part we've italicized. Does that sound like a commitment to empowering people?

The point is, the real or apparent dishonesty in the claim to be committed to empowerment on the one hand and to sell the program as a way to avoid investing in people on the other is a recipe for cynicism.

REVALUING STABILITY

At the risk of repeating ourselves, we're not suggesting for a moment that there aren't important changes occurring in society and in various markets. There are. And we're not arguing that organizations shouldn't change. They should. They have to. But we want to remind managers to stop for a moment to reflect on the value of the other side of the dialectic: stability, continuity, commitment, and loyalty.

Think for a moment about the value of permanence in the corporate identity. In their business best-seller *Built to Last: Successful Habits of Visionary Companies,* authors James Collins and Jerry Porras found that what was shared by the visionary companies they studied—ones they identified as successful over a long period—was an almost fanatical devotion to a "core ideology" or identity, and an active means of indoctrinating new employees into an ideological commitment to the company.[21] Niklas Luhmann, a German sociologist and philosopher, argues that organizations need a certain amount of closure and stability so they don't lose their sense of coherence and identity. Being responsive to the market is fine up to a point—but not at the expense of losing what's centrally important to the organization.[22]

Finally, we note that many organizations today look longingly for a dedicated workforce—while expressing surprise that years of change have led employees to reevaluate the very notion of career and to question whether they ought to get too personally invested with any organization. In other words, the idea of a social contract between employee and employing organization is now being renegotiated—on both sides.[23]

5

RESTORING THE BALANCE
BETWEEN CHANGE AND STABILITY

We have argued that the dialectic between change and stability is out of balance in popular and managerial thought today. All of us, in our work and nonwork roles, might be well-served to reconsider the degree to which we value change and seek more balance, recognizing that change and adaptability, although important for business and personal life, also have a downside, and that stability and routine have a valuable place as well. In this concluding chapter, let us offer several suggestions.

First, be sensible and self-reflective about the various fads and fashions that come along. Notice how others are marching under banners that may not be right for your organization. Or perhaps only some parts of a new trend apply to your organization. Certain functions may need to be reorganized as teams and others left alone—in the form of traditionally specialized departments. Think critically about the management language that everybody seems to employ. It's awfully tempting to let terms like *reengineering, outsourcing,* and *reinventing* roll off the tongue. Certainly they can be useful terms describing sometimes-useful concepts. But as we've shown, out-of-control change comes at a severe cost.

Second, choose your change initiatives carefully. Every time a new program isn't carried through to fruition, it raises cynicism. Always ask, "Are we willing to stay with this for a reasonable length of time?" TQM experts have suggested that organizations shouldn't expect positive results for five years after starting TQM. Five years! How many organizations are willing to stay the course on a change program that doesn't pay off for that long, especially in this age when long-term planning in some industries has come to mean looking just one year out, and stock values are eyed minute-by-minute? Yet, abandoning the commitment not only means that you're not realizing the benefits of the change being pursued but also means that you're creating skepticism for the next initiative. So, play devil's advocate. Have a second-chance meeting to ask, "Do we really want to do this? Do we have the reserves of energy and will to sustain our commitment to it?" If the answer is no, focus on improving current practices rather than abandoning them for the unknown.

Third, listen to employees' concerns about change fatigue, and develop sensitive and realistic responses to them. Involve employees early in the discussions about possible changes when you can so that they will have some influence in accepting or rejecting ideas or in managing the consequences. Accumulated research shows that employee involvement and participation in the formative stages of new initiatives—such as TQM or a broad customer service orientation—can make a big difference in the success of a program as well as improve it.[1] Also, engage in dialogue with other stakeholders, including representatives of stockholders, consumers, and the community.

Fourth, be attuned to ironies, contradictions, and paradoxes. And try to be aware of which changes your own initiatives have set in motion. Be critical of change scenarios offered by management books or change seminars, and use the experiences of your co-workers to develop your own interpretations of the future. Also, acknowledge the limits to any predictions.

Fifth and finally, recognize that your organization can be a setter of trends and not just a follower of the crowd. This is especially true for large governmental agencies, big private corporations, and major universities. But the idea applies as well to smaller organizations that should remember their own power to innovate. It is important not to be so caught up in the change movement that you forget what good things you've got and the valuable lessons you've learned from experience.

Of course, there are many kinds of positive changes: from a change of scene for a person who goes on holiday to a needed revolution in a country where the population is oppressed. Distinguishing between beneficial and disastrous (or even just more-of-the-same) types of change is not easy, however. Furthermore, even the best-laid plans of managers and activists often go astray. To pursue balance, we recommend that organizations periodically evaluate their basic activities and determine which they consider to be fundamental to their success or well-being or purpose. The criteria for assessing such aspects of the organization can include survival in the marketplace, consistency with basic principles or goals, centrality to the organization's identity, opportunities for advancement, and the various costs involved— economic, social, and environmental. In this way, organizations can keep the issue of change in perspective, making informed choices about areas where stability is paramount and others where exploration and experimentation are worth pursuing.

NOTES

PREFACE

1. Richard Sennett, *The Corrosion of Character: The Personal Consequences of Work in the New Capitalism* (New York: Norton, 1998).

CHAPTER ONE: THE GLORIFICATION OF CHANGE

1. James Gleick, *Faster: The Acceleration of Just About Everything* (New York: Pantheon, 1999), 12–13.

2. Peter Cappelli, Laurie Bassi, Harry Katz, David Knoke, Paul Osterman, and Michael Useem, *Change at Work: How American Industry and Workers Are Coping with Corporate Restructuring and What Workers Must Do to Take Charge of Their Own Careers* (New York: Oxford University Press, 1997).

3. Tom Peters, *The Circle of Innovation: You Can't Shrink Your Way to Greatness* (New York: Knopf, 1997).

4. Tom Peters, *Thriving on Chaos: Handbook for a Management Revolution* (New York: Knopf, 1987).

5. Tom Peters, *Liberation Management: Necessary Disorganization for the Nanosecond Nineties* (New York: Fawcett, 1994).

6. Michael Hammer and James Champy, *Reengineering the Corporation: Handbook for a New Management Revolution* (New York: HarperCollins, 1993); Bill Gates, *Business @ the Speed of Thought* (New York: Warner Books, 1999).

7. Edward E. Lawler, *From the Ground Up: Six Principles for Building the New Logic Corporation* (San Francisco: Jossey-Bass, 1996), 8.

8. David Osborne and Ted Gaebler, *Reinventing Government: How the Entrepreneurial Spirit Is Transforming the Public Sector* (New York: Plume, 1992), 11–12.

9. Jean-Francois Lyotard, *The Postmodern Condition: A Report on Knowledge* (Minneapolis: University of Minnesota Press, 1985).

10. Karl Taro Greenfeld, "Life on the Edge," *Time,* Sept. 6, 1999, 55–62.

11. Bush for President Web site [www.georgewbush.com].

12. Gore2000 Web site [www.algore2000.com].

13. Roman Laufer and Catherine Paradeise, *Marketing Democracy: Public Opinion and Media Formation in Democratic Societies* (New Brunswick, N.J.: Transaction Books, 1990).

14. George Cheney and Lars Thøger Christensen, "Identity at Issue: Linkages Between 'Internal' and 'External' Organizational Communication." In F. M. Jablin and L. L. Putnam (eds.), *New Handbook of Organizational Communication* (Thousand Oaks, Calif.: Sage, in press).

15. Xose Hermida, "Baudrillard Cree que el Mundo Se Ha Convertido en una Gran Disneylandia," *El País* (Spain), Sept. 28, 1999, 50.

16. Steven Covey, *Seven Habits of Highly Effective People* (New York: Simon & Schuster, 1989).

CHAPTER TWO: WHAT IS ORGANIZATIONAL CHANGE?

1. George Cheney, *Values at Work: Employee Participation Meets Market Pressure at Mondragón* (Ithaca, N.Y.: Cornell University Press, 1999).

2. Gregory Bateson, *Steps to an Ecology of Mind* (New York: Ballantine Books, 1972).

3. Karl E. Weick, "Educational Organizations as Loosely Coupled Systems," *Administrative Science Quarterly,* 1976, *21,* 1–19.

4. Terrance L. Albrecht and Betsy Wackernagel Bach, *Communication in Complex Organizations: A Relational Approach* (Ft. Worth, Tex.: Harcourt Brace College, 1997), 229.

5. William E. Halal, *The New Management: Democracy and Enterprise Are Transforming Organizations* (San Francisco: Berrett-Koehler, 1996).

6. Karl E. Weick, *The Social Psychology of Organizing* (New York: Random House, 1979).

CHAPTER THREE: ORGANIZATIONAL RESPONSES TO THE CHANGE IMPERATIVE

1. Lowell L. Bryan, Jeremy Oppenheim, and Wilhelm Rall, *Race for the World: Strategies to Build a Great Global Firm* (Boston: Harvard Business School Press, 1999).

2. Hedrick Smith, "Surviving the Bottom Line: Running with the Bulls," videocassette (Princeton, N.J.: Films for the Humanities and Sciences, 1998).

3. John Gray, *False Dawn: The Delusions of Global Capitalism* (New York: New Press, 1998).

4. Qi Xu, "TQM as an Arbitrary Sign for Play: Discourse and Transformation," *Journal of Management Studies,* 1999, *20,* 659–681.

5. Peter Case, "Remember Reengineering? The Rhetorical Appeal of a Managerial Salvation Device," *Journal of Management Studies,* 1999, *36,* 419–441.

6. Paul Hersey and Kenneth Blanchard, *Managing Organizational Behavior: Utilizing Human Resources* (Englewood Cliffs, N.J.: Prentice-Hall, 1996).

7. John Kotter, *A Force for Change: How Leadership Differs from Management* (New York: Free Press, 1990).

8. Lawler, *From the Ground Up,* 40.

9. Fletcher Challenge, news release, June 13, 1999. [www.fcl.co.nz/ home. asp]

10. Debbie Page, Ted E. Zorn, and George Cheney, "Nuts About Change: Multiple Perspectives on Change-Oriented Communication in a Public Sector Organization," unpublished manuscript (Hamilton, New Zealand: Waikato Management School, 1999).

11. Ravi S. Achrol, "Evolution of the Marketing Organization: New Forms for Turbulent Environments," *Journal of Marketing,* Oct. 1991, *55,* 77–93. See also B. Joseph Pine II, Bart Victor, and Andrew C. Boyton, "Making Mass Customization Work," *Harvard Business Review,* Sept.–Oct. 1993, 108–119.

12. Peters, *Thriving on Chaos.*

13. M. J. Zbaracki, "The Rhetoric and the Reality of Total Quality Management." *Administrative Sciences Quarterly,* 1998, *43,* 602–636.

14. John W. Meyer and Brian Rowan, "Institutional Organizations: Formal Structure as Myth and Ceremony," *American Journal of Sociology,* 1977, *83,* 340–363.

CHAPTER FOUR: CONSEQUENCES OF OUR OBSESSION WITH CHANGE

1. See "1999 Report on the American Workforce," U.S. Department of Labor, Washington, D.C. [http://stats.bls.gov/pub/rtaw/message.htm].

2. Sennett, *Corrosion of Character,* 22.

3. Holly Sklar, *Chaos or Community? Seeking Solutions, Not Scapegoats, for Bad Economics* (Boston: South End Press, 1995).

4. George Cheney, "It's the Economy, Stupid! A Rhetorical-Communicative Perspective on Today's Market," *Australian Journal of Communication*, 1998, *25*, 25–41.

5. Chris Galloway, presentation made at the annual conference of Australia–New Zealand Communication Association (ANZCA), Hamilton, New Zealand, July 1998.

6. American Management Association, Web site, July–August 1999 [www.amanet. org/periodicals/mr].

7. Price Waterhouse Coopers, press release, August 2, 1999 [www.pricewaterhousecoopers.com/gx/eng/about/press-rm/index.htm].

8. Sennett, *Corrosion of Character*, 49.

9. Sennett, *Corrosion of Character*, 24.

10. Gray, *False Dawn*, 1998.

11. Manuel Castells, *The Rise of Network Society* (Malden, Mass.: Blackwell, 1996).

12. Lars Thøger Christensen, "Flexibility as Communication. A Deconstruction of the Marketing Discourse of Organizational Change." Working Papers in Marketing No. 4, Odense Universitet, Department of Marketing, March 1996.

13. Joseph Schumpeter, *Capitalism, Socialism, and Democracy* (New York: Harper & Row, 1942).

14. John Cassidy, "The Firm," *The New Yorker*, March 8, 1999, 28–36.

15. Alvin Toffler, *Future Shock* (New York: Bantam Books, 1970).

16. Laurie Graham, *On the Line at Subaru-Isuzu* (Ithaca, N.Y.: Cornell University Press, 1995).

17. Helena D. Economo and Ted Zorn, "Communication During Downsizing: How Downsizing Survivors Construct Corporate Communication," *Asia-Pacific Journal of Public Relations*, in press.

18. David M. Boje, Grace A. Rosile, Robert Dennehy, and Debra J. Summers, "Restorying Reengineering: Some Deconstructions and Postmodern Alternatives," *Communication Research*, 1997, *24*(6), 631–668.

19. David A. Waldman, et al., "A Qualitatitive Analysis of Leadership and Quality Improvement." *Leadership Quarterly*, 1998, *9*(2), 177–201.

20. "What Does 'Employee Empowerment' Really Mean? Corporate America Puts $40 Billion on the Line to Find Out," Price Waterhouse Coopers press release, August 2, 1999 [www.pricewaterhousecoopers.com/extweb/nepressrelease.nsf/]; "Business Process Outsourcing Pioneer Joins Price Waterhouse Coopers," Price Waterhouse Coopers press release, November 4, 1999 [www.pricewaterhousecoopers. com/extweb/nepressrelease.nsf].

21. James Collins and Jerry Porras, *Built to Last: Successful Habits of Visionary Companies* (New York: HarperCollins, 1997).

22. Niklas Luhmann, *Essays on Self-Reference* (New York: Columbia University, 1990).

23. Vicki Smith, "New Forms of Work Organization," *Annual Review of Sociology,* 1997, *23,* 315–339.

CHAPTER FIVE: RESTORING THE BALANCE BETWEEN CHANGE AND STABILITY

1. Peggy Holman and Tom Devane (eds.), *The Change Handbook: Group Methods for Shaping the Future* (San Francisco, Berrett-Koehler, 1999).

DISCUSSION STARTERS

This booklet can serve as an excellent discussion starter for organizations, college classes, or your own private "salon." The following are some questions you could use to get things started:

1. How do you conceive of change? Does change happen to us? Do we cause it? Is change a wave we ride, a wave that washes over us, or even a wave we start or push forward? Is change a bandwagon that we jump on?

2. The messages about change that we get from the media and in our everyday conversations reflect and influence our attitudes toward change. Think of examples of such messages you've encountered. What do they say about contemporary attitudes about change? Do you agree with these attitudes? Why or why not?

3. What criteria can we use for discerning which kinds of organizational changes are inevitable, necessary, desirable, or optional?

4. Think of examples of organizations or managers who have articulated their plans for implementing change. What are their justifications? To what extent do they seem to assume that change for change's sake is desirable? What are the less obvious goals of their messages (for example, creating an identity of being dynamic or cutting edge)?

5. What does the notion *proactivity* mean to you? And how do you think proactivity is related to change—for an organization and for society in general? Do you think it is possible for organizations to be proactive while still serving the customer? Or are these aims mutually contradictory?

6. Many organizations that celebrate change are still able to remain stable. Think of examples of organizations that you know personally or through the media that do not seem to have any problem balancing change with stability. How does, or how might, your organization reconcile the tension between change and stability?

7. How can we revalue or reembrace stability at work without producing stagnant organizations?

ABOUT THE AUTHORS

THEODORE E. ZORN is professor and chair of the Department of Management Communication, University of Waikato, Hamilton, New Zealand. Previously, he taught at the University of North Carolina at Chapel Hill, after an earlier career as a corporate trainer and organizational development specialist. He teaches, consults, and conducts research on management communication practices such as leadership, facilitation, and change management. Currently, Zorn is incoming editor of *Management Communication Quarterly* and vice chair of the organizational communication division of the National Communication Association. He has served as a trainer and consultant for a variety of organizations in many industries and sectors.

LARS THØGER CHRISTENSEN is associate professor and chair of the Department of Marketing, University of Southern Denmark. He specializes in the study of corporate communications and has published articles and book chapters in the fields of advertising, semiotics, image/identity formation, managerial discourse, communication technology, public relations, and issue management. He is the author of *Markedskommunikation som organiseringsmaade: En kulturteoretisk analyse* (*Marketing Communication as a Way of Organizing: A Cultural Theoretical Analysis;* Akademisk Forlag, Copenhagen), which looks at the discourse of marketing and its implications for contemporary management and communication practices. Christensen frequently consults and gives seminars in the Danish advertising industry.

GEORGE CHENEY is professor and codirector of graduate studies in the Department of Communication Studies at the University of Montana–Missoula. He is also adjunct professor in the Department of Management Communication at the University of Waikato, Hamilton, New Zealand. Cheney's research and teaching focus on such topics as identity and power in organizations, workplace democracy, business ethics, and trends in public relations and marketing. He has published two books: *Rhetoric in an Organizational Society: Managing Multiple Identities* (University of South Carolina Press, 1991) and *Values at Work: Employee Participation Meets Market Pressure at Mondragón* (Cornell University Press, 1999). He has consulted with and provided training for a variety of organizations, including corporations, governmental agencies, educational institutions, religious groups, and social advocacy groups.

Together, the three authors are writing a textbook on organizational communication that will explore such topics as the unity of theory and practice, internationalization, and critical thinking about our most common assumptions regarding life in contemporary organizations.

B E Y O N D
T H E   B O T T O M   L I N E

*The prevailing economic orthodoxy has never been more in need
of questioning—which is why we're starting* Beyond the Bottom Line

NOW, MORE than ever, there is a need to question the received economic wisdom—the notion that the way things are is the only way they can be. Now there is a need to look beyond the bottom line.

Six times a year *Beyond the Bottom Line* will publish provocative, even controversial booklets that will challenge conventional economic thinking and point the way to a more humane, enlightened world of work.

Beyond the Bottom Line will tackle such issues as:

- Work and identity: Is what we do who we are?
- How can citizens gain more control over corporations?
- Are there hidden risks in the "New Science" and "Spirituality in the Workplace" movements?

Each *Beyond the Bottom Line* booklet includes a series of thought-provoking questions, making them perfect for sparking discussions in college classes, workplace lunchrooms, or your own personal salon.

The *Beyond the Bottom Line* booklets will be available individually, or you can subscribe to the entire year's run for only $49, a savings of 10% off of the single copy price of $8.95 (and if you subscribe, you don't pay shipping either—it's included in the subscription price—so you save even *more*).

A subscription to *Beyond the Bottom Line* will bring you some of the most iconoclastic and original thinking about business and economics to be found anywhere.

PREVIOUSLY PUBLISHED IN BEYOND THE BOTTOM LINE

Is Maximizing Returns to Shareholders a Legitimate Mandate?
Marjorie Kelly
Public corporations focus all their energy on maximizing returns to stockholders, often at the expense of employees, communities, even the environment. But as Marjorie Kelly demonstrates, there's no rational reason to do so. It's a form of discrimination based on property. It's aristocratic. And it's out-of-step with both democratic and free market ideals.
ISBN 1-58376-074-1   Item no. 60741-687 $8.95

**For more information about *Beyond the Bottom Line*,
visit Berrett-Koehler Communications online at bkconnection.com**

B E Y O N D
T H E   B O T T O M   L I N E

ORDER FORM

For fastest service, order online 24 hours a day through our secure server at
www.bkconnection.com • Call toll-free 7 AM to 12 Midnight: 800/929-2929
• Fax to 802/864-7626 • Or mail to Berrett-Koeher Communications,
PO Box 565, Williston, VT 05495

❏ Start my subscription to *Beyond the Bottom Line:* One year (six issues) for $49

Back issues: $8.95 each

___ BTBL #2: Do We Really Want Constant Change? *Theodore E. Zorn,
Lars Thøger Christensen, and George Cheney* (Item no. 60768-687)

___ BTBL #1: Is Maximizing Returns to Shareholders a Legitimate Mandate?
Marjorie Kelly (Item no. 60741-687)

Discounts available for purchases of 10+ copies of a booklet.
Contact Berrett-Koehler Special Sales for more information:
Call 415-288-0260, fax 415-362-2512, or e-mail bkpub@bkpub.com.

$_____ Subtotal

$_____ Shipping and Handling
($4.50 for the first booklet, $1.50 each additional booklet)

$_____ In CA add sales tax

$_____ Total

METHOD OF PAYMENT

❏ Payment Enclosed   ❏ Bill me P.O. number required _____

❏ VISA   ❏ MasterCard   ❏ American Express

Card No. _____ Exp. Date _____

Signature _____

Name _____ Title _____

Address _____

City, State, Zip _____

BILL TO (if different from ship to)

Name _____ Title _____

Address _____

City, State, Zip _____

Be the first to hear about new publications, special discount offers,
exclusive articles, and more! Join the Berrett-Koehler e-mail list!

Your e-mail address _____